SPACE STATiON ACADEMY

DESTINATION:
MERCURY

SALLY SPRAY AND
MARK RUFFLE

First published in Great Britain in 2023
by Wayland
© Hodder and Stoughton Limited, 2023

HB ISBN: 978 1 5263 2081 0
PB ISBN: 978 1 5263 2082 7

Editor: Paul Rockett
Design and illustration: Mark Ruffle
www.rufflebrothers.com

MIX
Paper from
responsible sources
FSC
www.fsc.org
FSC® C104740

Printed in Dubai

Wayland
An imprint of Hachette Children's Group
Part of Hodder & Stoughton
Carmelite House
50 Victoria Embankment
London EC4Y 0DZ

An Hachette UK company
www.hachette.co.uk
www.hachettechildrens.co.uk

The website addresses (URLs) included
in this book were valid at the time of
going to press. However, it is possible
that contents or addresses may have
changed since the publication of this
book. No responsibility for any such
changes can be accepted by either the
author or the Publisher.

Picture credits:
Page 30 Bill Ingalls/NASA; JPL/NASA;
page 31 NASA Goddard/NASA

SAFETY PRECAUTIONS

We recommend adult supervision at all
times while doing the experiments in this
book. Always be aware that ingredients
may contain allergens, so check the
packaging for allergens if there is a risk of
an allergic reaction. Anyone with a known
allergy must avoid these.

- Wear an apron and cover surfaces.
- Tie back long hair.
- Ask an adult for help with cutting.
- Check all ingredients for allergens.
- Clear up all spills straight away.

Contents

Meet the team

Dr Bott

Mo

Stella

Max

Xing

Melody

Welcome to Space Station Academy, the amazing interstellar school that travels through space. Come on board and learn about our solar system.

Today, the Academy is nearing Mercury. But before the students can get excited about that, there's been a delivery, and everyone has a parcel to open.

I've got new magnetic wheels! They fix to my body so I can move about on any planet, however weak the gravity, without floating away. I can use them today for our field trip to Mercury.

Amazing! I've got popcorn and sweets – we can share them.

In the classroom.

What do you already know about Mercury?

It doesn't have any moons.

It's a small planet – the smallest in our solar system.

Its diameter is 4,879 km, a third of the size of Earth and closer in size to Earth's Moon.

Earth

Earth's Moon

Mercury

It's a rocky planet, like Venus and Earth.

It's the closest planet to the Sun and it's hard to study from Earth because it's never surrounded by darkness.

As it is so close to the Sun, maybe I can wear my new sunglasses!

Good work, space cadets! Now, on with your space goggles and let's get ready to visit Mercury.

There it is! It's very fast.

Mercury travels around the Sun faster than all the other planets in our solar system, at 47.87 km per second.

It takes 88 days for Mercury to orbit the Sun compared to 365 days for planet Earth.

Imagine, we could have four Mercury birthdays in one Earth year!

We need to catch up with it. Scream to make us go faster!

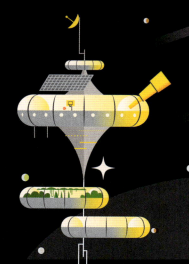

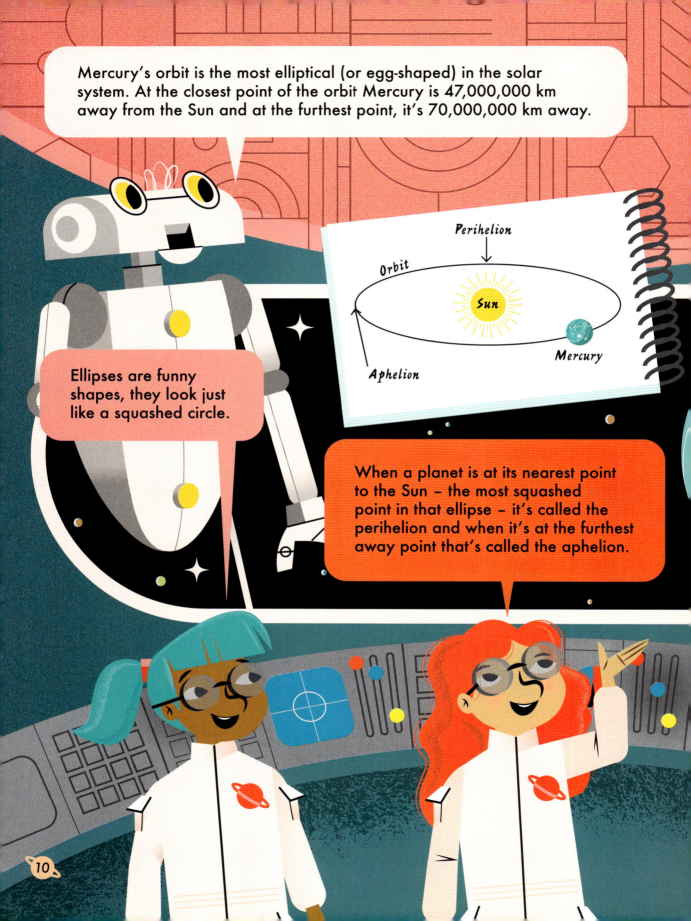

Mercury's orbit is the most elliptical (or egg-shaped) in the solar system. At the closest point of the orbit Mercury is 47,000,000 km away from the Sun and at the furthest point, it's 70,000,000 km away.

Ellipses are funny shapes, they look just like a squashed circle.

Perihelion

Orbit

Sun

Mercury

Aphelion

When a planet is at its nearest point to the Sun – the most squashed point in that ellipse – it's called the perihelion and when it's at the furthest away point that's called the aphelion.

15

Yes kids – let's go!

Hold on, I can't move! I'm stuck to the spot!

Oh dear, oh dear. My super-magnetic wheels are being pulled towards the molten iron and nickel core of Mercury! Over 70 per cent of the volume of Mercury is its core, which is proving to be highly magnetic!

Your wheels are not moving!

Push!

Take your shades off, Max! Then you can see where you're going.

The surface is covered in rocky craters and hills. It's been hit by loads of meteorites for billions of years. There isn't much atmosphere to keep them out.

We can talk to Dr B through my watch.

Dr Bott here! So far, 414 craters on Mercury have been identified and named. If a crater is over 300 km wide it's called a basin.

Formation of the Caloris Basin

The Caloris Basin is the largest. It's 1,525 km wide and surrounded by mountains, 1.5 km high. It was made by a meteorite hitting the planet. The impact was so big, it caused a mountainous area on the other side of Mercury, called the 'weird terrain'.

Get in and explore!

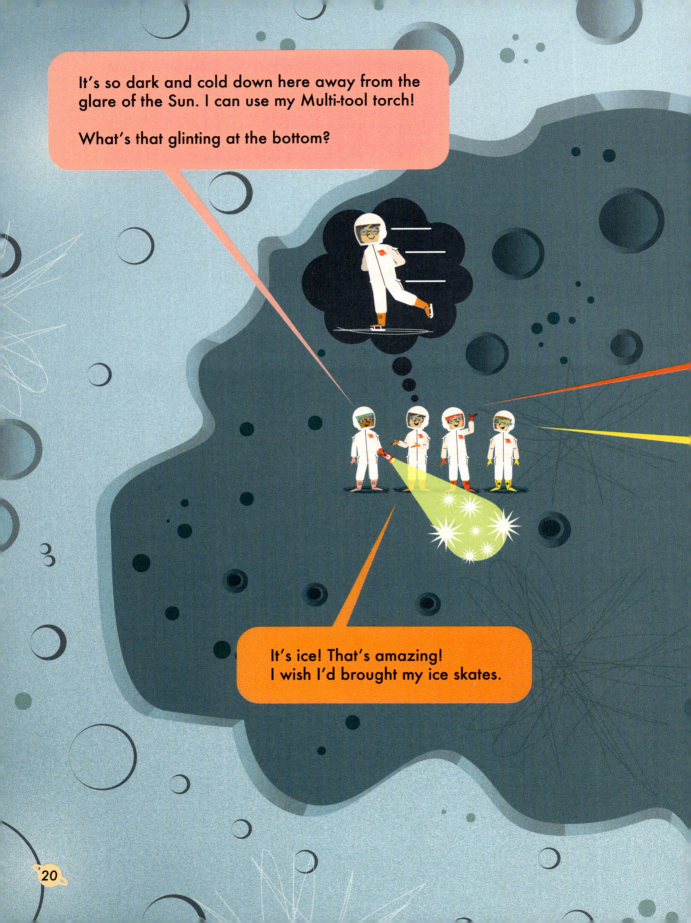

Oh good, you've found some ice! Ice exists in some craters on Mercury where it's deep and dark, shaded from the light and heat of the Sun.

It's amazing to think a massive meteorite made this big crater. Where did it go?

The impact made the meteorite vaporise into a cloud of dust. The dust then joined the rocks on the planet's surface.

Time to go! Back to the ship, everyone!

Back at the Space Station Academy.
Dr Bott is shopping for new magnetic wheels ...

Space Academy Activities

The Space Academy team have been so inspired by their mission to Mercury, they wanted to find out more. Will you join them?

Dr Bott's Space Experiment

Mercury is covered with impact craters. Have a go at making your own. You might want to try this outside.

Equipment
- Shallow tray
- Flour or cornflour or sand
- Cocoa powder
- Stones, shells, marbles
  - these will be your meteorites

Method
Fill a shallow tray with the flour or sand. Shake the tray gently to level it. Sprinkle a thin layer of cocoa powder over the first layer to make the surface of your planet.

Drop your chosen meteorites (stones, shells, marbles) onto the surface, one at a time, then carefully remove them to reveal your craters!

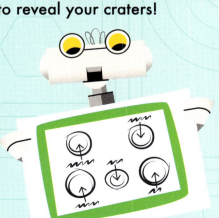

Outcomes
What happens when your drop the meteorites? What objects make the best craters? Make a map of your planet's surface. Name the best craters.

Experiment variations
Try using very light or very heavy objects to make a crater. What happens if your meteorite is an ice cube? How does the crater differ if the same object is dropped from a greater height?

Max's Mercury Fact

Did you know Mercury is actually getting smaller?! The cooling of its iron core is making the planet shrink and wrinkle. It's not going to disappear just yet; it took four billion years to lose 14 km from its diameter. Can you find out any other amazing facts about Mercury?

Melody's Collection

Make a rock collection like Melody. Mercury is covered in igneous rocks (formed from lava). See if you can identify the different types of rock you find and how they were made.

Xing's Maths Problem

You can have four birthdays on Mercury for every one on Earth. Can you work out how old these people are in Mercury years?

NAME – AGE IN EARTH YEARS

Xing – 10 years

Mo- – 26 years

Dr Bott – 54 years

Max's Grandma – 66

ANSWERS: Xing: 40 years, Mo: 104 years, Dr Bott: 216 years, Max's Grandma: 264 years.

Stella's Picture Gallery

Come and see the images in my marvellous Mercury picture gallery.

In this picture you can just about see Mercury orbiting across the Sun. Can you spot it?

Can you count all the craters on this small section of Mercury?

Mo's Research Project

Find out about past and future missions to Mercury. What can you find out about the routes they took to Mercury? What problems did the missions face and what are future missions likely to discover?

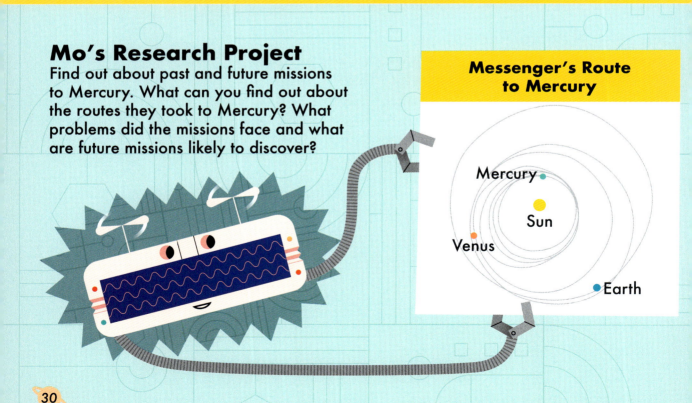

Messenger's Route to Mercury

Mercury

Sun

Venus

Earth

This is Caloris Basin, the largest crater on Mercury.

Here, Mercury is coloured to make the different features, minerals and chemicals on the surface stand out.

Further Information

Wonderful websites
nasa.gov/kidsclub/index.html
esa.int/kids/en/home
spaceplace.nasa.gov/all-about-mercury/en/
kids.nationalgeographic.com/space/article/mission-to-mercury

Brilliant books
Dr Maggie's Grand Tour of the Solar System by Dr Maggie Aderin-Pocock (Buster Books, 2019)
So Many Questions About Space by Sally Spray (Wayland, 2022)
Wonders of the Night Sky by Professor Raman Prinja (Wayland, 2022)

Glossary

atmosphere – the layer of gas surrounding a planet
core – the centre of something, such as a planet
crater – a large, bowl-shaped hole in the surface of something, such as a moon
diameter – the measurement across the middle of a sphere or circle
gravity – the force of attraction that pulls one thing towards another
interstellar – describes something that is located or happens between stars
magnetic – describes the natural force some objects have to attract or repel other objects
meteorite – a space rock that has fallen through a planet's atmosphere and landed on its surface
molten – melted, turned into liquid by heat
moon – a natural body that orbits a planet
orbit – to travel around a star or planet or the path taken around a star or planet
solar system – the Sun and the objects in orbit around it
terrain – an area of land and its features, such as hills and craters
vaporise – to change from a solid or liquid into a gas
volume – the measurement of how much space something takes up

Index